Conversations with Bibi

Conversations with Bibi

by

Alexa DeWiel

Some of these poems were previously published in:
This Magazine, Moving Out and Moving to Antartica.

Excerpt from "Here We Are", The Three Marias: New Portuguese Letters,
Doubleday Ltd.,1975.

ISBN 0-88961-019-3

Cover design and illustrations by Gail Geltner.

Published by the Canadian Women's Educational Press
305—280 Bloor Street West, Toronto, Ontario

Printed at The Coach House Press, Toronto, Canada

The design and production of this book have been the collective effort
of the author, illustrator and members of the Women's Press.

The author would like to thank the Ontario Arts Council for aid in writing
this volume.

...with thanks to Paulette Jiles

CONTENTS

A far ranging
shared circling round and round
this path we follow
to find sustenance

to sink firm foundations
for the dreamed of anchorage

where we now remain
separated from others
and yet so close

—Three Marias:
New Portuguese Letters.

DELPHINE

This one had paintings, they were meant to loom
much larger than herself

There where the elephants lay their heads down
under the trees,
she did not have lovers, she had paintings

She painted them either living •
or falling apart
She painted them with touches
missing or added

She tried fitting pieces together
and she tried blowing them up in coloured slides

These styles of expression changed little
from year to year until one year
she surprised even her
bony self and began to paint
great bodies
of water
in tiny tiny frames

Of salty silence her brain was a missile
suspended in liquid, grey matter no longer
fearful for its age,
these elephants down under the seas
rolled on like waves
tirelessly

tirelessly
amassing

These waves roll on like diluvial meditations
tirelessly

tirelessly
amassing

She brushed them not thinking of lovers and looming
and larger than painting,
her vital fluids, she brushed them with air, she
brushed them like fins on schools of fishes,
she brushed them like horses
down under the seas

These waves roll on
They roll on the heads, on the heels of populations
These waves roll on and they sleep alone
tirelessly

tirelessly
amassing

EASY STREET

Everybody's got their credentials hitched up good,
here on Fashion Central Easy Street

The owners ride around in their fat business bananas
Harmony floats in the air like money

> *every day day shift*
> *every night night shift*

Below the model suites sewing machines clatter
on and on no time for lunch break the women eat
their bread in silence beside the Christmasmink jacket
and in the bathroom
tell stories only other women would believe:

> *"He threw me on the bed*
> *and I was his,*
> *now I got love trouble,*
> *can't go before Jesus*
> *all dressed up in white"*

> *every day day shift*
> *every night night shift*

After six o'clock the sun goes down in orange
and red jags of glass splattered
across the parking lot

After six o'clock, the kids from over the restaurant
come out to play cowboys and Indians
leaping onto the baby's pram
in the empty parking lot

Rolls Royce pulls up to shoulder the day's take
and arrange next weeks's fur trade
with the sweet tooth cloth man with his silver cane
and cocky ascot polka-dot, bi-
sexual
Mr. I-can-make-it-on-the-phone inbetween the seats
kissing the driver, Mr. Two-
tone

Lost colours after infrared, sweatshops on Easy Street

Racoon coats to keep mama doing dishes all year round
on the hill back home in the outskirts of the city,
just her and the kids and the valium

You know she wouldn't be caught dead
in an old sweatshop working

        every day day shift
        every night night shift

MAKING MOVIES

Mosques are only for Muslims.
Mosques are only for men and boys.

There are no other women here like you and me.
North Americans walk with a different
brand of solitude, a big shiny disaster
stamped on their asses.

Spirit's frayed mythology.
Individuals groan: there is no message
                that is the message
                there is no home

...go with the flow...go to Mexico...Cuba...
go to India, go to Europe, Madagascar, just go...

Globally strewn sons and daughters
of capital gain—
vivacity begging for a piece of action
discarding clothes and worldly
wealth like bottles
like points of view

In Morocco the shuffle shuffle shuffle
of the daily life of Arabic feet
is continuous

Drink it all up,
mint tea at the foreigners' table;
small bowled pipes of kief are passed
around.
Ahmed and Jimi watch dozily out of the corners
of their eyes
as two Berber women scrub the kitchen floor clean,
their legs never bending over the tiles

Out in the street
a horse collapses in its traces,
overloaded
as you and I are supercharged
by travel

An old woman squats down on her heels
in front of me
rocking the family baby,
wrinkled
her breasts hang down

There are no other women here like you and me,
they're not as free,
coupled about town,
androgenized

Untroubled by the labours of the day
we sit by,
public as a bath.
Moviemakers wiping off our lenses.

I can hardly remember a word we said
all that year away
but a script arrived
like a long lost relative
after I had buried the reels

page by page
word for word

CONTINENT

Call us a liberated couple.
Nature takes its perfect course.

A couple of what? A couple of nations
posed in the lap of the sea-of-luxury,
the New World,
the cradle of content

I am a solid bowl of discretion
You are a melting pot of foreign affairs
containing all kinds of absolute reliance

Anyone can come in, it's an open marriage,
we have wide open doors,
it's our policy
to creep up on the wild life,
and generations learn,
children,
this is North America

What have we become?

Two countries, we are married by the land,
I populate you and then you populate me...

one excused the other for making a shadow,
rock impressions of itself in the lay of the land,
we have busy relations

He is passionate about money and figures
and she, she is a rich wife no less,
she got the goat, the kids, and the buckets of milk

They say she could become
a resort town
if someone would just
bust her wide open

In a murder there's a body to discover,
hover over delicately,
in a rape there's only the woman's words
and the economy of keeping quiet

And then suddenly there it is,
there it is:

    OIL OIL

'thar she blows and away they fly'
through the whole weary thing again,
the economic agreements;

As even the fearless sea whale
must one day give up its ghost
to the cheeky hunters,
so countries fall into each other's
enemy lines

Arguments in the kitchen all night long,
musclebound,
'the U.S. is a mess and just south of us'

We're strong, we hold our heads high
up here on cloud nine

Lock the doors so the neighbours can't get in
Lock the doors so the neighbours
can't get in like they used to:

Deportation is a free ride home

Overboard!

Foghorns please,
as we scramble
again
for the Good
Ship Patria

Foghorns please,
hot soups simmer
to a boil

Overboard!

The Church the Bar and the House of Commons
the church the bar and the house of commons

The crunch
Here everybody has a finger in the pie
She with her rip roaring temper
He with his electric grin

Mr and Ms
inscribed so nicely as partners
on the door of
National Development

Is it trains passing by
or arguments that rattle
the old neighbourhoods so?

In this agreement you only hear
what you want to hear
as the railroad races
from coast to coast

FAR FROM THE SEAT OF LONELINESS

*Why are you and I in revolt
against each other now?*

We ride bare back through the forest

swish swish swish

the branches

*Far from the seat of loneliness
lies a sand dune*

*which bears two rows of footprints
single file*

THE RECEIVER DANGLES

The receiver dangles
flaccid in my hands

your anger piles up
on my doorstep which I do not
scrub clean
like a meticulous wife

your anger
coils my hands into two claws
which ache to lacerate the bleak
geometric walls

Instead I drink
red, white, black

Why did you ever want me at all?

I have left you, now you
have nothing left, you scream
you could kill me for doing this to you

Always you envision the worst,
but I am not dead
I am not dead

Your mindlove leaks venom
I feel like your voodoo doll,
honey

SECRETARY

*Drums in the forest
echo
the counting machine
beat
their figures heavily
out on skin
from one metal desk
to one black telephone
to the next*

*Financial dips
common stocks
tom-tom comptometers
beat
until
Friday's deadlines
repeat themselves*

*beat
until the walls
fold in*

*beat until the laughing
time sheets crash
on top of me*

CAT AND GUITAR

Cats
blink
at the
feat
of
lighting
up

Ears
bend
backward
at the
sounds
of
twanging
cat gut
strings
colliding

MOONDOG

I fired Augustine's gun today.
Augustine shrugs it off,
says he's a byproduct of the war.
Industrious has nothing to live for now
he's out among the wounded, civies,
a fish out of water, casualty
flapping, no more
one dollar blow jobs in Saigon

Augustine and the broken hearted country boys
make veterans, they don't relax you
might as well be a sniper's mark.

 Hard nosed boy,
 you joined the army for something to do
 then you left the army because they used you
 and finally you caught the end of a manoeuvre
 Then you married a woman; you left her
 because she used you for security...
 now just because you're a man
 doesn't make you father to the child

People understand you, it's called deserted
it's called moondog

At night I kneaded your flat chest
You silently held back the reigning moments of sham,
the public outcry, the aftermath.
Then you leaked out everything,
so fast the sheets lay panting:

Questions urgently reloaded

SO THIS IS WHERE YOU LIVE NOW

What part of heaven did you fall out of?
The East End.
Don.
Who is this Don anyway?
Don River
Don Valley
Don Jail

So this is where you live now.
One door locks before the next one opens.
The pits. How romantic.
Sally Port and Dead Lock.
bev and vicky and mary jean.

Don't any of yous girls take my corner.
Roll your own and spit.
Modern Screen.
Laundry Room. Kitchen.
The corridors are lined with broads
waiting for the nurse to give them
their medication.
Bombed up. Wisdom's little nuts.

"That's what most of the girls do,
turn their face to the wall."

Yellow bellied cruisers cross
intersections casually radioed.
Two squad cars skid to a stop.
U Turns. Full charge ahead.
Bumper to bumper.
Rustling up the hustlers.

No visiting on court dates.
We offered her help but she wouldn't take it,
what can you do
      computer,
      issue issue

Where is your cup the one you were issued
      hack hack
superintent basher
      ward ward

That waxed mustache at the front desk
worked with matron for fifteen years
and never called her Julie
British Army
      momma goggle

MAY DAY

Another litter of kittens
has poured itself
blind baby five
into the old green
sleeping bag

five chirping heavy headed
five more mouths to feed

Mother cat purrs,
delivered of herself

A goldfish in a round dish
watches
her multiply

POCKETS

When cold nights preyed on each other
like the food chain,

without her rosie queenie,
she went hungry, she went back to Winnipeg

for deserts where everyone travels
too often there's nobody home

for voices you hear are the blue
blood voices of your loved ones

billowing into all the forsaken places
and overland, heavily as canvas

Some time passed and later,
so as not to let the boys down, she flew
back into town, high-risen Toronto,
to by and by the same
green felt tables
and matchless cues

Her lost weight became a relative
companion, appearing long legged
each afternoon through pool hall doors

three o'clock

They taught her tricks without rubbing
up against her side

the derelicts who could really tell
one clicky ball from another

She and they fingerpainted their desires
in steamy downpour ice over windows,
their registered convictions outran
each other into
melted fragile glass
containers
hailstorms

Eating only cigarettes,
they called city sounds obsessions
and country sounds silence

They let no hustlers put the make on her,
except for that red head, toscanini janis,
who kept flipping in the sunset
like a well baked fish

wild lookin' wimmin to be bop by

Without her rosie queenie,
she chalked up her own scores
like reckless graffiti,
a court stenographer
suspended from
the monarchy,
hand-me-down-decisions,
custodian of
welfare of
Indian summer of
empty lots of
vacant families

words are wanted to say but did they,
wives' tales
hearts' plunder

a singer when she sang
country blues, lonely like these
lines in past tense

CALM LAKE

Calm lake
  green grass
    yellow dandelions
    silver volkswagon
    denim jacket
      white running
      shoes, striped
      shirt brown
        bark
        dark
          green fir tree
            white strawberry
            blossoms
              blue eyes
                greenwater
                golden drum
              brown back
              black flies
            brown corduroy
            brown boots
          green passing car
        pink feet, red
        tail light
      patterned quilt
    yellow green moss
  brown wet hair
red insect crawling
on white birch tree

sleep now
sleeping one
beside calm lake

DAYDREAM SHE WOULD RATHER

She got up when she had to dry the clothes,
make tea,
move around while someone drew on her mind

She would much rather daydream than read
the news
She would much rather daydream than gather
her resources
take inventory
draw conclusions

Her friends told her she was buoyant
She knew she was sick of conclusions

She would rather sit and draw
tattoos,
leaves all over the floor,
hair, trees
and plain talk

She often flocked to the post office
for exotic momentos of many countries
Often there was a queen on the scene
and armies with acrid leaders

Many cats wandered in and out as she
daydreamed

Her friends told her she was reluctant,
proud, difficult to impress

She would fall into arguments fast,
fast like ink stains, like bee stings

Sometimes she wasn't much of a comfort

She thought about patriotism
and motherless countries while she drew

She always daydreamed when she looked
into the eyes of her beholder,
and if her beholder
was a sister,
then she daydreamed more,
because this gave her pleasure,
and principles

She loved their sensibilities
She had met some fine ones,
two in particular

She loved their sensibilities

Each was fine on her own but when they were together
Each was fine on her own but when they were together

She knew that brothers have been important
That there are very many
but she seldom believed them
She believed in divorces

Sometimes she wasn't much of a comfort
as a Catholic, difficult to try
in nineteen seventy-three

She preferred to come out
rather than smell like a rose inside
She lay, horizontally regarding the frontiers
of her rational suppositions,
oppositions
She knew she believed in no regrets

She daydreamed when she was looking
at new cars, remembering old cars,
upholstery and broad seats in which to lay out
her legs under trees, open window breeze

She had very many windows
Getting to know each of them better,
she watched them new
Sitting in the mainstream of a ray
she drew nude love from imagination
She had many daydreams

Thinking of one of them she would have to eat
Thinking of the other she kept her
mouth closed

She was different on the telephone
than she was off the telephone
Sometimes she spent days on the telephone,
depending on the time
and if she had it

Putting into it or pulling out of it,
this or that was always the question
She believed in the crisis of energy

She had very old cars
She always bought old cars and rode
around at night investigating neighbourhoods
and wondering if she could live there

One time she lived with two Catholic nuns
alone in a temple in Asia
There were many statues
There were few feast days
and many prayers

She left the Church
and wondered why action lies
only in the eye of the day dreaming
daydreamer

She daydreamed when she received postcards:

East is East and West is Aging Too

She laughed when she received
inhalations
She was a tentative receiver
She received but she was tentative
She had many daydreams

Of her intimate practices
like scratching
as she wondered why action lies
in the eyes of the daydreamer,
only a daydreamer knew who could let her
hear sounds like
chafing when there was only one
surface
and soft sighs when company was around

Sisterhood is not casual

She knew brotherhood to be important
but she seldom saw them
Given a row she found it difficult
to understand
what is hard to understand
between them

She had very good ears
She thought the true nature of walls
was keeping anything in or keeping
anything out
or anyone
or vases
or urns

She knew this because she daydreamed

Dreams are fondness recycled

Leaves caught in her hair
Sisterhood as usual
She had very many daydreams
She was careful with them

She'd rather
She'd much rather
Daydream she would rather

THE MUTE WILL BLOW

Long ago, longevity was assured,
hand planted in the hand that forbids
collisions, the seeds of peace—
    and for a thousand years the world
    lay pacific
    and warfare unknown

As the hills can tell you who remember
who for thousands of years have lain
like sleeping shoulders beyond the soft
and dark edged universe,
    every seed has its own finite time
    for escape and recovery
    from the amnesia grown out of times buried
    alive like lost
    residual cities

Decade after decade, her well watered
lambent eyes have watched these man-made
constructions, conquering erections
gathering momentum like contractions
for a stillbirth, native drums

Waiting, we have often had ways of thinking,
she knows more than she says, now its her
tune and still

we are an oasis of recollection,
you and I,
as
any lowslung moonbed will easily
collapse for travel
and a little change of heart

as we may often falter, I falter
we falter out of synch to our knees,
knots in our stomachs, helpless sights
and I might think there is no such
time as you, that I have created
you to be there for me.

In this war sometimes mistaken for peace
let us be steady and resourceful:
I have a pocket, you put something in it,
so everyone fulfills their dreams,
carries their seeds

And though generalities should be
left to generals
jumping through hoola hoops in the armed
forces, now dimly remembered like the illustrious
dead of a nation,
we must form a covenant because
we are not docile when we move.

We are borderless
We leave our marks low
like cows leave spotted calves

We call like hoot owls
across each others' hot spring bellies
we sow our seeds individually
We are an opening and a closing
as
echoes in the dark have ears will receive,
from warfare to pacific
a village of arms
together we will move
and then
the mute shall blow

LONG DISTANCE

I just wanted

to hear
the
sound of yourvoiceofyourvoice
the sound
of your
voice

   voice
       your voice
   of

   sh sh sh sh....

       Montreal

CONVERSATIONS WITH BIBI

In moments of ease we do alright.
Dried plants
hang everywhere.
Rustle in the night. Slung
around doorknobs. Tied behind photographs.
Jammed into closets.
Sumach sassafrass and mint.
Everywhere an herb cabinet.
A humble abode. The floors are slanted.
We like it because it's home.

There are many ways to be trailed to one's door.
You pursue I fly You fly I follow.

Questionnaire.
Do you speak French?
Une Autre Jour Sans La Femme.
Ah oui, c'est merdeaux, tu sais.

How are you.
I am simply that.
I pushed the door and it opened,
conversations with Bibi
can you imagine the feeling.

I cultivate your reply.

(Piano please)

Did you see me from afar.
Very afar.
You were the dragon.

(Piano please)

Solo flight for one moog
and again
the chant of ten saxophones

(devoted) (charging)

Some nights you play incredible music
conversations with Bibi
the way you attack the horn

Fire burns in its place. The fire. Place.
The food is simple and nourishing.

The problems are financial.
How to pay the bills.
Collateral. I married a broker.
Money was time. We bought and bought.

Then he sold insurance.
Trapdoor.
To be mesmerized by fate.
We transferred constantly from city to city.
      One day we floated away on an ice floe
      and came back magnets
      and came back mad

To bait to set on to bite or to worry.
Confined animals chew their paws.

Please sit down. God Save.
Oh Portfolio.
My gentle history.
Did you see me when I ran.
Did you see me stick it and shove it.
Did you watch the little dearie die.
Here is a bust of your revolution she faces you.

The Businesswoman Goes to Lunch.
Look at my new briefcase, I found it in the dump.
All it needs is some stitching,
Frugality.

I hate always grubbing for money.
Don't go. Sometimes I see you all unhappiness.
Must you pose for a living.
Don't you.
Too fat too thin. Too much head in Glamour Magazine.

She rose to bring back
a painting she had never finished, the figure
of a woman squatting in front of a brick wall.
On her lap
the heads of two seals who lay
on either side of her,
dry dry,
water nowhere to be seen.
Title: She Breaks the Whole Thing Up.

I thought I heard someone knocking
but it was only a fragmentary
interruption of her own
conversation with someone like herself

Conversations with Bibi
seek sanctums

Weekdays you can hear birds whistling.
Tractors digging out the gravel pit.
Two big crushers and a link belt chain.
Construction workers singing arias:
Maria Maria

Sap's up.
I make a footprint.
Blades radiate.
I make a footprint.
Blades float in wind.

We were tired of the chit chat.
High quality wilderness experiences advertised.
White power consummation. Get it while you can.
A poster for your wall.
The turn of a phrase. A curious conceit.
Image banks. Neodata showcases.
Industries of inventions recorded by professionals.
Row by row.
Tiptoe through the volumes. Do not bend the files.

But a butt. Look alive doll.
You more pure than the driven snow.
There are many ways to be hounded.
Lose track.
Don't stop don't think go crazy.

I make a footprint. Far from the convent.
A long train of thought.
We escaped
Thanks.
Three chants in a row.

Conversations with Bibi
connect night to morning
branch to leaf.

Daily

It was a short summer but a long
and leisurely fall. Lingering
on the unfinished kiss on the unfinished lip
of the unfinished painting.
Lingering electrical dashes. Visual acoustics.
Flashes. Acupuncture meridians.
Feel mine back there. Over to the left.

Riverwill circulate the news.
This is Sunday. Sundays are more.
They are slow and easy.
We don't have to answer the phone. Do we.
Don't.

Conversations with Bibi
when one head nods two can too

Dance together in the kitchen chair.
Loaves and blankets make the world go round.

A full moon helps. To say what does not come
easy as Sundays these days
without resounding trite.
To know what it is to say my dear
my most darling darling.
To know what to do with time.

It will stop your heart
if you can't go on.

You can go on.
Talk other languages in your sleep.
Leaflet. Other meanings.

And the river is deep
red is the colour of the
banks of the river

Mornings the fields are wet.
We open the gate.
In the daily life of the daily living
there are ten worlds in each a thousand
and
conversations with Bibi
continue.
Long afterwards.
I make a footprint.

I HOLD YOU

I hold you
like a little fish
or a baby
or clouds

I hold you
like a little fish
or a baby
or clouds

I hold you
like a little fish
or a baby
or clouds